RUMI

A NEW SELECTION

RUMI

A NEW SELECTION

TRANSLATED BY

FARRUKH DHONDY

HARPERPERENNIAL

An Imprint of HarperCollins *Publishers*

First published in India by Harper Perennial 2025
An imprint of HarperCollins *Publishers*
4th Floor, Tower A, Building No. 10, DLF Cyber City,
DLF Phase II, Gurugram, Haryana – 122002
www.harpercollins.co.in

2 4 6 8 10 9 7 5 3 1

P-ISBN: 978-93-6569-153-5
E-ISBN: 978-93-6569-367-6

Typeset in 11/15 Bell MT at
HarperCollins *Publishers* India

Printed and bound at
Thomson Press (India) Ltd

MIX
Paper | Supporting responsible forestry
FSC® C010615
FSC www.fsc.org

This book is produced from independently certified FSC® paper
to ensure responsible forest management.

To the memory of my friends Firdaus Ali and Mahmoud Jamal

CONTENTS

INTRODUCTION

Jalal-al-Din, born into the family of Baha-al-din Valad of Baksh in the northern territories of the Persian empire in 1207, later known as 'Rumi', is today the bestselling poet in the United States of America. This is an astounding fact, as he wrote his revered, and now translated, volumes of verse in Persian, with smatterings of Turkish and Arabic. Astounding, because the sales of his books in American translation surpass those of William Shakespeare, John Keats, Walt Whitman, T.S. Eliot and other canonical writers writing in English.

Why? Rumi's great work, the 'Masnavi', is sometimes dubbed 'the Quran in verse'. It certainly is devoted to Islam, but to a version and interpretation of Islam with a long and widely adopted history loosely referred to in all its variations as 'Sufism'. The doctrine of his verses absolutely conforms to this spiritual interpretation of the Quran and the Hadith—the exemplary acts and sayings of the Prophet Muhammad. It is not just a matter of conjecture that the vast majority of the people who have made him one of the most widely read poets in America are not followers of Islam or any of its sects. Of course, some of the fans of his poetry—and I would count them on the total fingers of a baseball team—are scholars of Sufism. The majority know nothing of Islam or of its demands and disciplines.

They, and their imitators and counterparts in the rest of the world—Europe and India—don't know the Quran. They are devotees of an interpretation of Rumi's verse as a doctrine of mystical self-realization and of 'love'. This last word is open to historical evolution of its meaning.

Rumi's verse doesn't celebrate explicit Romeo and Juliet interaction. The 'love' it celebrates can never be interpreted as the desperate emotion one has for the girl in the graduation prom or for the girl next door. It has nothing to do with the celebrated romantic longings of Hollywood or, for that matter, of Bollywood. The love expressed in Rumi's works, the six volumes and twenty-four thousand verses of the 'Masnavi', his *Diwan-e-Shams* dedicated to his inspiration and 'lover' Shams-u-Tabrez, and in his discourses and lectures, is a dedication to the divine. This 'love' in his poetry is not something one feels sexually for the person dated through the internet and cultivated as a being worthy of sex and dedication, it is a metaphor for an abandonment to what Sufis consider the infinite, the source of life itself. When Rumi openly professes 'love' for his inspiration and spiritual partner Shams-u-Tabrez, it's not an expression of a gay relationship, but rather a metaphor for a divine bond, a union of individual souls in a universal soul.

If the followers of Rumi in the West, inspired by the prolific 'translations' of his works realized this absolute truth, would they turn away from the misrepresented Sufi-Islamic message of his verse?

JALAL TO RUMI

Depending on which account you read of Rumi's life, he was born Jalal-al-Din Valad in 1207 in Baksh or, more likely in the smaller town of Vakhsh where his father Baha-al-Din Valad was an Islamic scholar, preacher and teacher of Islam with a dedicated following of pupils. Baha-al-Din was of the Sufi and ascetic inclinations of Islam and was vociferously opposed to the narrower judicial doctrines. This brought him into conflict with the leaders of judicial Islam, the kazis and other officials who had, in his own estimation, denied Baha his rightful rank in the hierarchy of Muslim clerics.

The disagreements and indeed disputes led to Baha taking his family, with some of his disciples in tow, to Samarkand—today in Uzbekistan. After a few years in that city ruled by the descendants of Barlas Turks, Baha-al-Din and his family moved further West within the Persian diasporic kingdoms of the time. The Persian kingdoms spread at the time from the borders of Baluchistan, through what we now know as Iran, north and east to Uzbekistan and Afghanistan and westward into Anatolia, now part of Turkey.

Though the city of Konya in Anatolia was ruled by a Persian king called Ala al-Din Kaikobad, it was referred to in the general argot as part of 'Rum', the Roman empire which had, governing from Constantinople, dominated the region through the previous centuries.

Baha-al-Din died in 1231. Jalal was twenty-four years old and would be considered by his father's students and followers—most of whom may have been older than him—to be not quite the teacher to succeed their respected Mowlana.

Jalal-al-Din may have been too young to lead a theology class, but wasn't, by custom and tradition too young to have married Gowhar Khatun at the age of seventeen and fathered two sons by her.

Baha had specified that Jalal was to succeed him as the Mowlana of the institution which was a madrasa and a congregating hall for Sufis. Since it was evident that Jalal would not command the respect of this congregation, it was agreed by Jalal to send for one of Baha's star pupils Borhan-al-Din to hold it in trust for Baha's designated successor. Borhan was at the time teaching in Kayseri, but in deference to the memory of his late mentor, agreed to fill this vacancy till Jalal was deemed fit to take on the responsibility.

It must have been Borhan who suggested that Jalal go to Damascus in Syria and enrol in one of that city's famous madrasas to study for a degree in Islamic sciences and theology. When he obtained his degree, he returned to Konya and studied the works of his father and of Borhan himself. It was this study that deepened his devotion to the Sufi teachings, though those were certainly initiated in his boyhood by his father.

In time, Jalal assumed the role his father's death had left vacant and began lecturing in Konya at the Sufi academy, leaving Borhan free to return to his duties in Kayseri. Reports speak of his prowess and power as an exponent of the spiritual path of Sufism. He is supposed to have gained several professorial positions in Konya and his lectures and courses were, apart from the scholars who dedicated themselves to Islam, attended by merchants, artisans and by men and women alike. The dedication was not, in this phase of Jalal's preaching, to his final Sufi doctrine as propagated by Shams-u-Tabrez who had not yet entered his life.

Even the teachings of Baha and Borhan interpreted Islam—the subservience to God—as the constant quest for unity with Him. It was certainly a profound and mystical departure from juridical Islam, which stressed the duty of the Muslim to pray five times a day, to follow Sharia law and go through, enact and participate in the prescribed rituals. (The contemporary interpretations of Juridical Islam, influenced by the teachings of the eighteenth century preacher Abdul Wahab, have led to the formation of organizations such as ISIS, which justify the genocide of unbelievers and heretics).

And then Shams arrives in Konya and confronts Jalal in 1244. Jalal is now thirty-seven years old.

Very much of what is written about Rumi is myth. There are two prevalent stories in this vein about his first encounter with Shams-u-Tabrez, who then became his guru, master, transforming catalyst and 'lover'.

The most popular story is that Jalal-al-Din, having succeeded his father as the teacher of Sufistic Islam to his students and followers in Konya, was lecturing before them. Beside him on a table was a pile of books—learned works on Islam to which he referred and his pupils were required to study.

His lecture was interrupted by the unannounced and unexpected entry of a tramp-like, or at least a wandering-dervish, figure. Rumi, distracted by this unwarranted intrusion, paused in order to perhaps challenge the intruder, but before he could ask this person—who was, of course, Shams-u-Tabrez—to leave, the intruder pointed at the pile of books and said 'What are these?'

Rumi contemptuously replied, saying in effect, 'Nothing that the likes of you would understand.'

As he said this, to his astonishment and that of the audience in the room, the pile of books burst into flame. Astounded, Rumi must have backed off from the blaze saying, 'What's going on?'

Shams then coolly replied. 'Nothing that the likes of you would understand.'

Shams then leaves the lecture theatre and Jalal, intrigued by what he presumed was a miracle worker, follows. He catches up with Shams down the street.

The myth then goes on to say that no one knows what transpired between them, but the two of them were locked in conversation for forty nights and days in Jalal's segregated quarters, after which time Rumi emerged with the essence of Sufism in his mind, on his lips and in his pen.

The metaphoric intent of this 'myth' is obvious. Shams is a mystic and enters a scholastic lecture to change philosophical discourse and the texts on which it is based, if it doesn't contain the essence of advanced mystical Sufism—which is suspicious if not condemnatory of dry Islamic scholastics and aspires to devoting oneself entirely to the quest for unity with God.

Setting the books on fire is the symbolic rejection of this scholasticism. As a 'miraculous' occurrence it proves that the mystic has powers beyond those that Rumi and his pupils and followers understand. The intrigue then is the key to the search for enlightenment and, as in all Sufi teaching, the guide to realization is a teacher, a master—or as Rumi puts it in his verses—a 'King'!

The number of the forty nights and days may or may not be an allusion to the life of Issah, Jesus, who according to the Bible spent forty nights and days in the wilderness and emerged with the message of God, which he went on to preach to the world. The Quran and consequently Rumi in his verse, constantly refer to Jesus the miracle-worker and the miracle in himself, so it may be perfectly justified to see the allusion to precisely forty days of enlightenment in this context or through this comparison.

That the myth doesn't attempt to explain how the transformation of Jalal-al-Din to Rumi took place during those forty days indicates that the reader of his verse must learn of it from the expression of the Sufi enlightenment rather than its mechanism.

There are variations on this myth perpetrated by different scholars and chroniclers after Rumi's death. The closest to the above story substitutes water for fire. Rumi is sitting by a pool of water when Shams intrudes on his studies and puts the same sort of question to him, pointing to the books Rumi has by his side and asking, 'What are these?' Rumi replies with the same supposed contempt, saying, 'They are intellectual and philosophical debates, not for the likes of you!' At which point the books miraculously fling themselves into the water. Rumi reacts with consternation. The books are singular and precious. Shams miraculously retrieves each book from the pool and there's no sign of any of them having been in the water. Rumi of course leaves them by the pool and follows Shams into enlightenment.

The metaphoric myth relies on the same shock of a miraculous immersion and a retrieval of the philosophical tomes without them being affected by the miracle they have been the victims of. It seems to point to the fact that the enlightenment that

Shams is bringing to Rumi is beyond the teachings or convictions of those scholarly treatises.

Another quite different myth of the meeting of Rumi and Shams portrays Rumi as a lecturer in a college to which a peddler of sweets—of 'halwa'—comes. Rumi asks him for a sample of his sweets and the peddler, Shams, hands him one morsel, which Rumi eats. The peddler doesn't sell or give any more of his halwa to anyone but departs, followed by Rumi who then disappears for years and only returns to Konya repeating unfamiliar, inspiring verses which his pupils hear and learn by heart and then record in what is left to posterity as the central work of Rumi's life, the 'Masnavi'.

The symbolism of this myth is the morsel of enlightenment which Shams feeds to Rumi alone, leaving him to return enlightened and pass on the conviction or doctrines of Mevlevi Sufism to the world through his works. And naturally, the morsel Rumi absorbs is in the metaphoric form of the favourite Persian sweet.

The story that's perhaps closer to the historical truth is that of the first philosophical encounter of Rumi and Shams. Even that is sometimes set in a mythological framework. One account says that

Rumi was riding a donkey through the streets when Shams blocked his path, grabbed the bridle of the donkey and posed philosophical questions to Rumi who answered in a way that Shams didn't expect but was respectful of and sparked their immediately blazing relationship.

The more factual account involves the invocation by Shams of the figure of the ninth century mystic, Bayazid Bestami. Bayazid was an Islamic mystic who is sometimes referred to as an early or pre-Sufi believer. The account of the first encounter says that Shams approached Rumi, in the street or wherever else, and challenged him with the question 'Who is the greater—Bayazid or the Prophet Mohammed?' Different accounts pose the question in different ways, but the challenge to Rumi is the same.

Rumi's answer is that Mohammed is infinitely greater because he professes to continually seek God, whereas Bayazid claimed to have attained a unity with the infinite and claimed that he was part of that infinite and therefore had attained union with the divine. Mohammed's quest was that of the humble supplicant. Indeed, the word Muslim means one who prostrates himself/herself in humility. Shams judged Rumi's answer to make him worthy of being a spiritual companion and their 'union' begins, according to the legends, in this way.

Shams-u-Tabrez has left in his *Maqalut*, a sort of autobiography, an account of his interaction with Rumi. He seems to say that he had encountered Rumi in Damascus, after the death of his father Baha-al-din Valad and before Rumi succeeded him as the Mowlana, the professor-preacher of Konya. In an intermediate period when Rumi was not old enough to take his father's place, he called on Borhan-al-Din, a disciple of his father, to lecture in Konya. Burhan sent the young Rumi to Damascus to further his studies in theology. It was there, according to Shams that he first encountered Rumi and was impressed by the young man's knowledge and interpretations. Shams writes that they didn't exchange more than a greeting at that point, but only fifteen years later made the acquaintance that would alter Rumi's entire religious outlook and give the world his poetic works.

On reading Rumi's works and his pronouncements on his relationship with Shams any reader would get the distinct impression that the man he calls the master and the king and his lover is the superior or at least guiding partner in their relationship.

When Shams disappears from Konya, threatened by Rumi's pupils who are bewildered by the change in their teacher's stance and demeanour, Rumi mourns his departure and represents it as heartbreak and ultimate loss.

And yet the account of their relationship by Shams himself in the *Maqalut* paints a different picture. Shams expresses deep respect for Rumi's acumen, learning and intellect and specifically says that there was no question of him being the master and Rumi being the pupil. He does go on to say that Rumi's reference to other scholars' philosophising would get in the way of his progress towards the oneness with the infinite that Sufis seek.

I only came across Shams's very detailed description of his relationship with Rumi on reading the masterful and comprehensive work *Rumi* by Franklin D. Lewis, Associate Professor at the University of Chicago (*Rumi: Past and Present, East and West; The Life, Teachings and Poetry of Jalal al-Din Rumi* published by Oneworld Oxford—and this is by way of acknowledgement of this extensive scholarship).

Shams writes about entering Rumi's household. Rumi, after the death of his first wife Gowhar Khatun, the mother of his two sons, marries a younger woman. Shams says that according to Sharia law and Islamic custom of the thirteenth century, a woman was not allowed to be in the presence of a man who was not her husband. And yet, Shams says, Rumi had no objection to his young second wife sitting at the feet of Shams and listening to his discourses.

The transformation, which contact with Shams brought about in Jalal, was not acceptable to Jalal's congregation and possibly not even to his family. Jalal emerged from their prolonged and private discourses with what he claimed was true spiritual enlightenment. His religious conviction had taken the form of self-abnegation in the interests of union of spirit with the 'master' and through him with the Infinite. The forms of communication changed from logical discourse to mystical realization in verse and song and even in dance.

It is perhaps through this transformation, when Jalal begins to compose verses in ecstatic form, that his appellation came to be altered from Mowlana Jalal-al-Din to 'Rumi'.

For some of his pupils and followers, this transformation was perceived as a defiance of lucidity and something close to blasphemy. It generated amongst Rumi's congregation a deep antagonism to Shams.

Threatened by this hostility, Shams left Konya and disappeared. His absence was acutely felt by Rumi, whose muse, it seems, had departed because as is evident from the chronological evidence, he wrote very little at this time. Finally, news reached him that Shams was in Syria in Damascus and Rumi sent his son Sultan Valad to go there and persuade him to return.

The persuasion and the assurances must have worked as Shams did return to Konya.

By this time, the hostile disciples of Rumi realized that his transformation and dedication to the form of ecstatic Sufism that Shams had brought to him would not change. Things wouldn't go back to what they were before Shams-u-Tabrez entered Konya and their Mowlana's spiritual 'understanding'.

By this time, a year or more since his reappearance in Konya, Shams had taken a young woman, Kimia Khatun who had been brought up in the Valad household, as his wife.

This wife died soon after and the disciples and even Rumi's family members accused Shams of neglecting his young wife's health, which led to her death.

It was perhaps this episode which culminated in threats to Shams's life, which resulted in his second and ultimate flight from Konya. Though Rumi initiated searches for his whereabouts, he never found Shams. It is likely that he had been murdered and the body disposed of as he disappeared without a trace.

By the time of Shams's disappearance, Rumi had written a substantial number of ghazals to him. Through his period of despondency and grieving for Shams, Rumi expressed his love for Shams by beginning to write the *Diwan-e-Shams*, a book dedicated to his inspiration and a gateway into this selfless spiritual quest.

By all accounts, Rumi felt the need for a master, a *shaykh* through whom his devotion to God could be expressed. After Shams's disappearance Rumi adopted Salah-al-Din Zarkub as this figure. Salah-al-Din had been a disciple of Borhan, who in turn was a disciple of Baha-al-Din, Rumi's father.

The myth of Rumi's first encounter with Shams says that they retreated to the house of Salah-al-Din for six months and carried on a discourse. They had neither food nor drink during this time and the only person allowed into their presence or perhaps into their discourse was Salah-al-Din. So, Rumi's transference of 'love' from the now absent Shams to Salah seems natural.

In this period, Rumi composed several ghazals to Salah. Their philosophical relationship lasted for ten years till the death of Salah. In the few years after, Rumi began work on his magnum opus the 'Masnavi', often referred to as 'the Quran in verse'. By the time of Rumi's death in 1273, the 'Masnavi' is complete and is one of the main sources, the largest oeuvre of Rumi's poetry in translation.

Many verses in the *Diwan-e-Shams* and in the 'Masnavi' speak of the merging of souls or spirits. Rumi says that their Sufi conviction and pursuit has been a merging of the spirit—to roughly paraphrase (unpoetically): I am you and you are me and there is no me and you because we are one in that merger.

THE SECTIONS

Whilst adhering to strict metrical patterns and to rhyme (with reason), Rumi wrote his verses in many forms.

I've chosen four distinct categories of Rumi's verse and present them in four sections:

The first is a selection from his very many Rubayii. These are four-line poems with each line in iambic pentameter (the meter in which Shakespeare wrote most of his plays three hundred years later) with the first, second and fourth lines rhyming. Very many Persian poets have used this form and Edward Fitzgerald stuck to it in his beautiful rendition of Omar Khayyam's *Rubaiyat.*

Rumi also wrote in the ghazal form—a Persian poetic discipline in which the second lines of successive couplets rhyme in two syllables: for example—in a completely frivolous invention:

When you look into my eyes, I feel them pierce
My soul and know you're looking through me

I fell in love with you when you in generosity
Gave me that translation by Farrukh Dhondy of Rumi

And if I find that I've copied some of his lines
I'm sure his publisher, his agent and he will sue me…

The second section of these translations have taken some of Rumi's philosophical ghazals but not attempted to strictly follow the ghazal form as attempting it in English could appeal as a mechanical and pedantic effort.

The section contains philosophical poems, very many of them devoted to his union with Shams-u-Tabrez, taken from the *Diwan-e-Shams.* These are headed by the numbers of the verses in that work.

These are the heartfelt expressions of the Sufi philosophy of the dissolution of the self and the merging into the Infinite—through the beloved, the friend, the king, the moon, the sun—all symbols for Shams who is the leader into—to borrow a term from Buddhism—the Sufi nirvana.

Some of the verses are addressed directly to Shams-u-Tabrez. In others, he is represented by the conventional Persian poetic metaphors of the time—the saki: the dispenser of wine, the moon that illuminates the dark, the garden, the light ...

The third most extensive section includes my translations of the parables that Rumi composes in his 'Masnavi'. These are all narratives with lessons and a moral. They are in most cases more extensive than the parables of Jesus Christ recounted in the New Testament. In many of them Rumi makes biblical references to Issah, Jesus, adding to the testimony of Matthew, Luke, Mark and John. Rumi's parables, engaging narratives, are all in the service of one or other Sufi lesson or moral. They follow the pattern of telling a story to make an ethical, moral or theological point. Rumi was undoubtedly familiar with the teachings of Issah, but that is not to say that his parables were composed using those of Jesus as precursors or models. Telling a story to make a moral point is part of the pre-Christian culture and tradition of very many Eastern civilizations, including Persia.

The parables are perhaps the least abstract of Rumi's methods of instruction. This section contains stories of people, of animals, of dramatic progress that can illustrate a moral. Some of the parables are self-contained stories with their moral implicit in the action. In others, Rumi interrupts the flow of the narrative with interposed philosophical injunctions, some short and some extensive, before returning to conclude the narrative.

What may startle the contemporary reader is that Rumi doesn't hesitate to use words which today would be asterisked. In these narrative poems, he uses the Persian words for sexual organs without euphemism—though their inclusion is directed towards compelling morality.

The final collection of this translation is a section devoted to the pithy and singular aphorisms taken from here and there from Rumi's oeuvre. Each of these provokes a reaction which can be personal and always leads to the universal. What do I mean? As translated here—as accurately as such transference allows—each aphorism can be embraced as a personal guide and injunction or as a universally illuminating thought. Two random examples:

Wisdom tells us that we are not worthy
Only Love can assure us that we are
The one leaves you feeling you are earthy
The other elevates you to a star

Our yesterdays have melted with the springs
Today is new so say, please say, new things!

Of course, the Sufi doctrine would say that the personal is the universal as long as the ego dissolves and merges with the Infinite—the route being 'love'—whatever connotations that word contains, hides or rejoices with.

Rubaiyat

1

Your love infused my frozen heart with fire
My conceits turned to ashes on that pyre
I left all sterile learning on the shelf
And danced to the melodies of desire.

2

O Rabab, singing minstrel of the dunes,
Before your melodies my poor heart swoons
You are desire's spy, whispering sands
The secrets of the heart are in your tunes.

3

The Beloved is my eternal sun
And I, the lover, like a planet run
In orbit round him and when springtime comes
And branches sprout, I am the dancing one.

4

The infidel declared that 'God is dead'
And yet the sun is nucleating red
Glaring down on denouncers on the roof
Who close their eyes to wonders He has bred.

5

Your silence was replaced by moral tales
So song, replacing piety, prevails
When you without a name shuffle the pack
And toss the coin to predict heads or tails.

6

Why you left me I will never know
I was less than nothing to you and so
More loyal to me than you ever were
Is this longing for you—O let it grow!

7

You accept me and yet I am afraid
This fear is that my allure will fade
Or is it that I know the evil eye
Is in my shadow, lurking in my shade.

8

You won't even grant me a single glance
I think that's sinful, but you take the chance
To ignore every heartfelt overture
Will nothing induce you to change your stance?

9

I begged the physician 'Prescribe a cure!
This is a suffering I can't endure.'
He asked me where it hurt, I took his hand
And touched it to my ribs where it felt sore.

10

The day I stood outside the tavern door
I cast off all disguises evermore
The passers-by all sought their destinies
Was I alone questing my inner core?

11

I tell the Saki I don't need her wine
I'm happy in myself as I am mine
When mortals say 'no future awaits me'
I say 'to have no future is divine'.

12

This sorrow does not recognize this blight
Itself is blind and thinks I have no sight
We see the stars reflected in the streams
Can anyone venture to steal that light?

13

Lamp of the night I urge you not to sleep
Shine bright O moon and penetrate the deep
Darkness that surrounds all the universe
As crescent or as orb your promise keep.

The night was dark, the moon came out to play
But steeped in darkness all that I could say
Was 'leave me now I am averse to light.'
And thus we mortals turn fortune away!

14

The flood will drown my poems and my songs
This disguise returns to whom it belongs
So now exposed my sins and sorrows stand
The moonlight will dissolve my rights and wrongs.

15

Love is the power that sets hearts aglow
Its energy can soften rocks and so
Don't criticise the sins of lovers who
Are captive in its tide of to and fro.

16

My turban, robes and everything I own
Are worth less than the false dirham that's thrown
Into the dust and into oblivion
No face, no signature, a name unknown.

17

Within a cloud lightning and thunder roll
Only loving eyes see the sunrise whole
His presence is an ocean in my heart
All creation is submerged in his soul.

18

So, pluck these strings, the rabab of my heart
Play melodies of distances apart
And though it's ruined, love remains within
Thus even ruins inspire works of art.

19

O dance and whirl, the melody now swells
The tambourine and flute's rhythm compels
Longing defines itself now as desire
And breaks out in a thousand plangent yells.

20

The thorn lives in harmony with the rose
No terror on the moon can night impose
The buyer and the seller are as one
Love's companionship is all Rumi knows!

21

Unlike King Suleiman I'm a worm
A lover of love—though that makes some squirm—
My only gift now is my broken heart
Infected by love's variant-breeding germ.

22

You found my true self when you ripped my veil
And burning me in love may yet entail
Awareness that the passing of my years
Is nothing if this youthfulness prevail.

23

Worship and sin perceived as the same thing
Are as in the tavern a saint and king
Merging in dissolution with one face
With orbs of heaven illuminating!

24

The day I die my soul will go, I trust,
To heaven though my body turns to dust
Yet if your hand bids me to rise again
I'll leave the grave and the faithless non-plussed.

25

A grain of salt, I dissolved in the sea
No faith, no scepticism bothered me
The heavens are already in my heart
Where God resides and Love is his decree.

26

By poetry my spirit was beguiled
A thousand fragrant maidens drove me wild
In every verse their allure would appear
Like virgin Miriam pregnant with the Child.

27

My joyful soul from its confines is torn
Moving to new resorts with every dawn
Like currents leaving static banks and rocks
So each new day a new story is born.

28

You'll find peace when you're rid of every need
When you to pomp and status pay no heed
When pain and sorrow both just pass you by
When from every atom of Self you're freed!

29

Nothing is hidden from the King—He knows
Though your heart's cry in utter silence grows;
Let poets turn their sorrows into words,
I serve Him who can heed my silent prose.

Philosophical Poems

Mostly from

Diwan-e-Shams

BLISS

Young man why would you fall in love like me
Sunken in sorrow, high in ecstasy

Obsessed with every contour of his face
Whose brightness is for you a warm embrace

Trusting in him, I surrendered it all
The world, my friends, even my ego's thrall!

As oil in water rises to the brink
Just so I live with the crowd, distinct

This freedom from desire leaves me pure
Its madness no physician can cure.

That same physician infected with this
Madness would burn his books and thus find bliss

Abandon everything, The Source entreat
As biscuit mixed in milk can make it sweet.

TURBULENT WAVES

Within my soul there rose turbulent waves
Echoes of oceanic rants and raves

Cast off all possessiveness if you can
The slave's then master of this caravan.

I dreamt I was cast into poverty
It enveloped, embraced and transformed me

Keeping me in its trance until the dawn
Demonstrating the beauty it could spawn

I drank in that dream a red ruby wine
And I was clad in a gemmed robe divine

I heard the din of lovers and their speech
The clinking of wine glasses, each to each

These were all adrift on poverty's waves
And wore in each ear rings of poor slaves

In that dream the light of poverty shed
Visions of the living who were dead

Poverty's voice in that moment began
To tell all slaves they owned the caravan.

154

O ugly face you cursed me in the street
The vulture's breath always stinks of dead meat

Your filthy words were aimed at my disgrace
Their vile nature reflected in your face.

You speak of death and all is enmity
Yet my Friend, the Beloved, protects me

The ocean pounds the shores through light and dark
Oblivious to this foul dog's bite and bark

Mecca flooded with infidel tourists
Is still the Holy City—that persists!

In all mirrors the face of Yusuf shines
And yet a stranger in that frame reclines.

The shadow of a bat upon the sun
Can't pretend that its brightness is undone

Issah laughed when his cousin Yahya frowned
From doubt—though Issah was the truth profound

The people asked Allah 'Which of these two
Should we follow upon the path to you?'

Allah said 'follow my dictated creed
Refrain from sinfulness in word and deed

The doubter doesn't doubt out of fear
He is the victim of the insincere

Pride and gloating—these the roots of sin.
The gates of hell open to let them in.'

The enemies of the moon live in the dark
Eternal shadows which never embark

As birds from trees when the dawning arrives.
They are like bats, the devils of the skies

Shunning the light into the dark they fly.
How long does the mote remain in the eye?

280

You and I—those moments full of joy
You and I in unity destroy

The distinctness of bodies in one soul
You and I—distinct forms and still one whole.

We enter the garden of You and I
As songbirds spill their music from the sky

In love our separateness is undone
The garden's beauty is we two as one.

The stars of heaven will shine on us soon
Then You and I shall be the night sky's moon

Our merging hearts have absorbed You and I
No idle fable tells you how or why

Like sugar cracked by heaven's parakeets
Our Union is to us heavenly treats

This togetherness defies time and space
We're here at once and in some other place

Such as Iran, Iraq or Khorassan—
In this Garden and yet in Hindustan!

And in one form upon this blessed earth
And in paradise through this second birth.

TO THE SUN

Call on the Sun to fill the world with light
Shed joy on friends—and on enemies blight.

And mountains, lamps and rocks incarnadine
Like rubies—make sour grapes yield sweet wine

O Sun! Shine down to make all gardens green
Let festive angels in the fields be seen

O lantern of the heavens find the cure
So love's wounds may be healed for evermore.

Don't veil your beautiful face with a cloud
Shift the veil, smile upon us blithe and proud

Hiding your face condemns us to the dark
So set our days alight, O heaven's spark!

292

You sprang out of my heart into my sight
Chanting a profound spell that shed a light

On all creation. And then with one breath
You encompassed all being and life and death.

A single penitence washes all sins
But does the loser even know who wins?

Ayub and Yakub with you do reside
Which means Love shall ever with you abide.

Enter the cemetery do not despise
The crumpled corpses, command them to rise

And join together in a joyous dance
Turning away from fate and circumstance.

I speak of what I can clearly see
This isn't some outrageous fantasy

If someone says 'I've fled the world and gone,'
Say, 'You will recognize him from his torn

Garments.' In silence now respect sorrow
Of the Beloved. Don't seek to borrow

Answers to the quest. Let the silence speak
And tell the questor 'This is what you seek!'

301

Your heart has become hard as granite rock
Impenetrable now it seems to mock

My entreaties. I feel I am but glass
Utterly shattered by the rock, alas!

Just like the dawn you've chased the stars away
Announcing with your laugh the birth of day

Love opened up its bosom to embrace
Me—and transport me out of time and space

And when Patience witnessed my ecstasy
It mounted a horse and then followed me

And thus both Patience and Reason depart
Leaving just Passion and a weeping heart

Starved of the Master's captivating wine
The herd lingers by the roadside like swine

Through its spell Reason becomes a stranger
The broken heart stays locked in its manger

Love is the pure substance of His command
Poetry the music of its demand

Leave Loneliness and Separation's theme
They inspire words which can only scream!

O Imam flee the mosque, those prayers forget
O Muezzin come down from the minaret!

340

Escaping through the narrow cage's eaves
You've fled this unjust planet full of thieves

You scrubbed the mirror till the glass was clear
And looked upon the image of the Seer

You've heard the voices of the high and low
You've seen what you have seen and now you know

Water and clay are substances of earth
Which through you are granted spiritual birth

You lived beyond your body and life's change
You revolutionized all spirit's range

This mother's womb we call 'life' is a whim
You have attained the Wisdom we call Him

Constantly fill his cup, Saki make haste
With sweet wine wipe out this life's bitter taste

Take all the world it's yours for you to choose
You've chosen us, we've nothing left to lose.

You emerged from the pot of life a sweet
And now you sweeten all the world's conceit.

The bird has flown and left an empty shell
You fled this world in spirit to excel

Through every moment you achieve increase
Fly yonder, your wonder will never cease

Death has provided the key to your lock
The silence that's the key that none can block!

345

Springtime brings me laughter and I sink
As though last night I had too much to drink

The moon has wrapped me circled in its light
I found The Friend—now there's no
'friend' in sight

The lute's melodies set me vibrating
You hear the music, but can't see the string!

He stirred the world up like a stormy gust
And then He vanished like the settling dust

That King set me on fire with his spark
Then like a spark he vanished in the dark

In gardens of the heart he was the Rose
But did the thorn ultimately dispose

Of the brightest pink blossoms on the stem
From envy of sharing a life with them?

My heart says 'Tell the Saki now before
I leave the tavern, pour me just one more!'

Mirrors reflect but never ever speak
I ask the mirror's holder 'Shall I seek

His beauty that's reflected in the glass
Timeless beauty that shall never pass?'

The Sultan's falcon in this moral story
Tells us that every victim has its quarry!

316

Sea water has satiated the sand
It hasn't covered me, so here I stand

No string is long enough to thread my bow
It will remain quite harmless, unstrung so!

No sea is full enough to quench my thirst
No mountain relieves this hunger accursed

I am a Leviathan full of grief
O God how and when will I find relief?

More thirst than all-encompassing death
I get more ravenous with every breath

The lean lover's salvation is to merge
Your feeding hand satisfies hunger's urge

You trapped all reason and chopped off its head
And shamed its pretension—yet it's not dead!

Your sincerity was your faith and church
Your images mirrored each human search

Noah defied the flood and built a raft
The scent of your spirit can drive men daft

Return then to the Palace of no sound—
Silence and Love can make The Lost The Found.

123

At sunset as the night prayer is pronounced
In the Unseen the senses are renounced

Spirits are driven by angels of sleep
As the shepherd who drives a flock of sheep

To spacelessness and spiritual meadows
Through gardens and cities the spirit goes

In sleep the Spirit from our world escapes
And sees a myriad mystic forms and shapes

Perhaps the Spirit had origin where
There was no memory of this world's care

That place was ever the Spirit's abode
Without life's heavy burden or its load.

46

Come gather friends, this is no time to sleep
Sleepers cannot the law of The Book keep

In turning imitate the water wheel
The garden's face shall then itself reveal

If your heart yearns for earth's water and clay
The river's dry and all earth washed away!

O moon of my heart's sky, come out to play
So no traveller can deny it's day

Let me not know where The Beloved's gone
The day, for Him, my heart stops beating on

SONG

You are my song, my wished-for melody—
You enter into me, a spacious sky
Through which the gentle wind flows constantly
Where silence sings the song of you and I!

Sow seeds in my heart, cover them with earth
The magic of your hand will prove fertile
The ground will spout, this drunkard's careless mirth
Sing through those lips of the perpetual smile

FLAMES

It's love that sets lovers alight
They burn in passion through the night

The royal seal of romance graces
The grand throne of their embraces

Sunlight brightens lovers' windows
I am dust dancing where the wind blows

Welcome to the feast of desire
Fire-eaters to the feast of fire

These flames are mirrored in the sky
Infinite stars as far as the eye

Can see—they are all heaven's flames
So many we can't give all of them names!

SHAMS

My cup of wine is shattered
And all the wine is gone
My body and mind are tattered
The cure relies upon

Shams-u-Tabrez the Prince
The guide to all true seeing
The one who can convince
The drowned soul into being

Alive above the ocean—
With celebrations on the shore
Music, festive commotion
Laughter and wine to pour

Where trumpet sheds a ray of light
Where sight and sound are one
Only Shams bestows this delight
There is no other—none!

Shams is the energy that sets,
Like strong winds overhead,
Moving atoms in streams and jets
Tasting of salt and bread

Seek for yourself the borders
Fly with wings, depart
And tired with obeying orders
Lie down and open your heart!

THE SEASON

Feel lucky now you hear the melody
Of flutes approaching down the dusty roads
They invite dancing feet, the feast is set
The earth itself in a deep glow explodes!

And through the night we'll sit sipping sweet wine
Because it's spring: a spreading, glowing sea—
We hover above it, clouds in the sky
Or floating on the ocean—its debris.

Seeing the oceans thus, I know I'm drunk,
And in Spring's intoxication I laugh.
In the night sky you see me shoot a dart
Towards the moon and split it into half!

LEARNING WORDS

As mothers can both chastise and embrace

Their babbling babes who're just learning to speak.
A thirsty man runs to the sea to seek

Relief from longing though he knows it's cursed—
Salt water can't relieve a human's thirst.

The jealous lily staring at the rose
Suffers the fate that beauty does impose.

I am the tambourine whose beat imparts
The rhythm when the frantic dancing starts

So hold me and continuously shake
Me. Silence in the dance is a mistake.

Yusuf is most beautiful when he's nude
Revealing the glow with which he's imbued.

When I am dead, my jaw shut finally
From its dead-silence will come melody.

LOVE BESTOWS

Love bestows on lovers the gift of flight
They fly heavenward to the realm of light

And through this flight they tear a hundred veils
Destroying illusion, the truth prevails

The first step is to renounce life and gain
That second life granted to the insane

The last step is the step into nowhere
Where enlightened feet dance upon the air

Regard this world invisible and see
That wilful blindness will set your Self free

I said 'O heart, may that endeavour bless
You to enter the world of love's caress

Your eye has a range that sees far and wide
And yet it penetrates substance inside

The windings of the bosom. Say from whence
Came, O my Soul, this rapturous intense

Breath into my breast? What sorcery apart
From love's embrace brings throbbing to my heart?'

BE

Be a lamp and illuminate the dark
Be a lifeboat, imitate Noah's ark

Or be a ladder, elevate a soul
With prospects of love's heights to make hearts whole

Or be a shepherd, help some souls to keep
Through Shams's Grace the innocence of sheep.

POETRY AND EXPERIENCE

Beware my friends the hazards of poetry
It sets in metaphoric words a snare
It imparts the illusion you have been
In moods and places, though you were never there!

376

O Melody I embrace you—you bring
Signs from the spirits whom you taught to sing

You strike the ear and pass into the soul
You move nature and cause the rocks to roll

You rise through bodies and take hearts aloft
Your heart is loud, your dance and footfall soft

You are the moon caught laughing as you shine
As though you are drunk on heavenly wine

Your fragrance bears evidence of repast
On sweet honeyed nourishment first to last

O Melody, you fertilize the earth
And give the thrusting blades and blossoms birth!

Parables from the 'Masnavi'

THE MUSLIM AND THE ZARTHUSHTI

Two friends, a Muslim and a Zarthushti
Had from childhood lived in close amity

The first turned to his friend, meaning no harm
Suggesting he should convert to Islam

The Zarthushti replied 'If God commands
I shall of course comply with his demands.'

The Muslim said 'Allah wishes you well
Converting to Islam saves you from hell.

So, say the words and give your soul relief
Though your ego persists in disbelief.'

The Zarthushti then replied to his friend
'This thing called ego compels me to bend

To its wishes and if God controls all
The Universe, my ego's in his thrall.

Nothing, we know, happens without His will
Then why, if He ordains all, am I still

A Zarthushti? He leaves us to decide
What's true or false—from Him no soul can hide

The dictates of free will are his bequests
To humans to believe as they think best.'

The Muslim decided not to retort
They both sat sipping coffee in deep thought.'

MADNESS AND PEACE

The famous Egyptian sage called Zolnoon
Was surrounded by disciples and soon

Felt pressure by their eagerness to know
The secrets of the universe and so

As more and more disciples joined this quest
Poor Zolnoon surrendered his mental rest

And soon it became evident to all
That Zolnoon's brain, thus crowded, was in thrall

To fits and unhinged irrational states
Which panicked his disciples and his mates

Who expressed their concern that Egypt's best
Sufi philosopher faced this unrest

Of mind—which emerged as most foul abuse
And formulations obscure and obtuse

Sometimes he'd even throw violent fits
His disciples then said to each 'It's

Time the Master had a prolonged rest
Perhaps a sanatorium would be best.

And that was how they shut Zolnoon away
From the turmoil of each questioning day

So Zolnoon now isolated in peace
Felt a calm descend on him—a release

From all the turmoil of rational strife
He settled into a routine of life

Of reading Islamic Sufi treatise
Which brought his frantic brain a newfound ease

His disciples, however, thought they should
Visit Zolnoon to ascertain what good

This exile and this solitude had done
But Zolnoon in this retreat wanted none

Of those he concluded had made him mad
So when they came to visit, Zolnoon had

Made up his mind that he would act insane
To test their loyalty as true or vain.

When they came he let out some foul abuse!
They didn't suspect this was Zolnoon's ruse

To gauge the love and friendship they professed
So Zolnoon contrived an ultimate test

He ran screaming from them and grabbed a rock
And hurled it shouting 'You who've come
to mock

Me in this place and keep up the pretence
That I'm insane and you are blessed with sense.'

He threw more stones pretending to be vexed
His disciples just stood, confused, perplexed.

Zolnoon continued his bizarre antics
Pelting them with stones and even with sticks

This behaviour was too much to endure
And so the 'friends' decided to withdraw

And Zolnoon shouted 'Call yourself my friends?
A friend is someone whom nothing offends

I was play-acting, true friends would have guessed
But in your falseness you have failed the test.'

As they fled he gave them a dirty look
And returned to his 'Friendship Treatise' book.

A DONKEY'S BURDEN

A donkey, a poor water-carrier's slave
Was whipped and tortured to make him behave

Without complaint all through the
stretching day.
The skins of water on his back would weigh

Him down as he was forced to circulate
Around the villages whose thirsts ordained
his fate.

The poor creature forced to work so hard
Was starved and whipped and so bodily scarred.

One day as he was forced down the main street
His master met a friend and paused to greet

Him. This old friend looked at the poor beast
And said 'For God's sake, friend, you could
at least

Feed this poor animal some proper food!'
He added then, 'I don't mean to be rude

But let me volunteer to help of course
I'm now the Master of the Sultan's Horse

I'll take this poor creature into care
I'm sure in due course he will prosper there.'

The donkey's master readily agreed
Business was slack, he wouldn't have to feed

This beast of burden—at least for a while
He accepted this offer with a smile.

The friend then took this drudge into his care
And to the Sultan's stables where he'd share

With studs and mares their meals of
luscious hay
At first he thought 'How has this come
my way?'

But then this creature began to compare
His state with theirs, which led him to despair.

Disheartened he turned to God to complain
'These pampered creatures never feel the pain

I've suffered all my life. Creator why
Have they been granted luxury and I

Have been condemned to hardship? Is this fair?
They're fed and flattered while I've had to bear

Skins of water and carry those loads
Down alleys and down never-ending roads?'

His constant complaint covered the same ground
And as he rambled Lo! There came a sound

Of trumpets summoning the troops to war
And as they blared, soldiers began to pour

Into the stables with saddles and swords
And rode the horses out to face the hordes

Of enemy troops invading the land
This cavalry went out to take a stand.

The donkey wondered what was going on
His stablemates were saddled and were gone.

A few of them by morning stumbled back
Retreating from the enemy's attack

With arrows wedged in their flesh through the war
Our donkey was aghast at what he saw:

Horses with battered limbs and blinded eyes,
Horses, their neighs of pain were louder than the cries

Of tortured souls in hell. The donkey cried
'O God forgive my not being satisfied

With the place you allotted me in life
I won't henceforth look upon it as strife.'

In time he left the stables and went back
To carrying the water-skins and pack

Knowing that God and Justice have their schemes
And destiny is never what it seems.

YUSUF'S FRIEND

Yusuf had a very close childhood friend
With whom, when they were young, Yusuf had shared
Adventures and a pillow from which they'd tell
Each other stories. They really cared

For each other. Alas! They grew apart
In different towns, but after years had passed
This friend travelled to visit Yusuf's home
And thus the pair were united at last.

The friends wanted to catch up and find out
What had life brought the other over years
Of course, the friend had heard about Yusuf
But knew truth was always fouled by rumours.

He asked what he'd felt when he knew
His brothers were jealous and planned to sell
Him into slavery after they held
Yusuf prisoner inside an empty well.

Yusuf answered frankly—he said 'I felt
Like a lion with its neck in a chain
Which didn't degrade me because I knew
That God's plan was I would henceforth regain

My dignity and that my brothers would
Bow down to me and beg for forgiveness.'
'And the time when you suffered in prison?
That was the key to despairing, I guess?'

'It wasn't,' Yusuf replied, 'Like the moon
I was confident I'd be full again
Or like seed-pearls powdered for medicine
I'd cure the sick and achieve wholeness then.

My friend think of me as a grain of wheat
That grows to become flour and then bread
To nourish someone's body and their soul
Consider me that grain of wheat instead.

Or think that I felt like the planter's song
He sang at night after he sowed the seeds
What my ten brothers did to me was wrong
I knew they'd seek forgiveness for their deeds.'

Yusuf changed the topic and asked his friend,
'Knowing our customs, you must be aware
That travellers bring gifts to please their hosts
So tell me, my friend, what presents you bear

For me and this household, I'm pretty sure
You wouldn't leave a grind-stone without wheat
And God will ask the same when you ascend
What have you brought to flatter my conceit?'

This guest, embarrassed, did apologize:
'Yusuf you know, I wouldn't dare to come
To see you empty-handed but I must
Admit I didn't dare to bring some crumb

To your grand sumptuously supplied table.
Nothing seemed appropriate: why take gold

Into a goldmine. Or a cumin seed
Into Kermanshah from where cumin's sold?

Should I take drops of water to the sea?
I can't even gift you my love and soul
—You already own these since we were young
I've brought you one gift that contains the whole

Being of our love and our unity.'
So saying he brought out what he'd concealed:
A mirror which he handed to Yusuf
Adding 'Gaze in this all will be revealed.'

He meant being and non-being are one
The gift of anything else would be vain
Let the mean gaze on generosity
The reflection of bread is hunger's pain!

If you hold up your sins the mirror shows
An empty blankness asking to be filled
By efforts of all human art and craft
To obliterate all that is self-willed!

A tailor works on garments that are torn
Carpentry involves chopping down of trees
The doctor's skill needs broken limbs to heal
To be cured identify our disease!

Let your vileness be reflected and weep.
Consider Satan's flaw, his vanity
Asserting he was Adam's superior—
Consider that crude sin's insanity!

An open wound attracts a swarm of flies
A cover like your self-protecting sense
Word from a Master can drive them away
Your healing is this Master's recompense

As through the bandage light will enter you
And demonstrate that false is also true.

SOUND OF A SLAP

A man was sitting on a narrow bench
When at his side he felt somebody wrench

Him towards the seat's edge to make space
Even though the seat was designed to grace

Just one human bottom comfortably.
But before this man could look up and see

Who was nudging him, he felt a tight slap
Behind his neck, resounding lie a clap.

The slap made his neck violently burn
But before he could possibly return

The blow, his young assailant blurted 'Please
Before you slap me back may I just seize

This moment to ask you about the sound
My slap on your neck made, you're bound

To have heard it. I really have to know
If my palm gave off the sound of the blow

Or was it the skin of your neck that screamed?'
To the man who'd been assaulted it seemed

He'd met a fool. He shouted 'You're insane!
Asking stupid questions when I'm in pain!

Idiot, have you nothing better to do
Than wasting people's time? The likes of you

Should be locked up—you're a shameless disgrace.'
He stood up from the bench and left that place.

What moral from this tale must we infer?
He'd left the bench to the philosopher.

CONSIDERATION

A friend once asked the Prophet why it was that
He always lost in business deals because

People with whom he deals would cast a spell
With sums and figures so that he can't tell

What the agreements are and what is worse
He thinks he suffers from distraction's curse.

The Prophet replied 'Why not stipulate
That every business decision must wait

Three days for you to think and then agree?
Deliberation is the only key!

When you throw your dog some little titbit
He'll sniff it to ascertain if it's fit

For him (or her) to countenance and eat—
So just like the dog you must be discreet

God created the universe in six
Days, even though we know that he could fix

All creation by just pronouncing 'Be!'
So why not follow God's example? He

Provided us with Prophets one by one
Over ages to see his will was done

Issah awoke Lazarus with a word
The Word from God over his lifetime heard.

Consider the current of every creek
It pushes here and there trying to seek

Its passage through the mud and rocks to flow
And patiently to Mother Ocean go.

The bird emerges from the egg, it's born
Quite unlike the womb from which we're torn.

Consider us with brains and hearts and feet
All humans but each of us quite discrete!'

DESTINY WINS

King Suleiman the prophet nicknamed 'wise'
Would every day hold a public assize

His subjects would approach him with their woes,
Complaints, demands for justice, even those

Which questioned edicts Suleiman had passed.
One day a distraught, ragged being cast

Himself before King Suleiman in court.
So the king asked him what justice he sought.

The ragged man who seemed quite out of breath
Said 'Lord, I've just seen the Angel of Death

Outside here, he was waiting in the street.
Staring at me, my heart refused to beat.'

Then Suleiman said 'We know Azrael
Guides souls who die, to heaven or to hell

God instructs him and Azrael obeys
Now dear man I can discern from your gaze

A strong panic, what would you have me do?'
The man replied 'Salvation, Lord, is you

I beg you now my life is in your hands
Convey me from his reach to other lands.

Send me to Hindustan, so I won't face
This Azrael, Angel of Death's embrace.'

Suleiman agreed and called the East Wind
'Convey this poor individual to Hind.'

That done, Suleiman began to address
Other citizens seeking some redress.

The next day when Suleiman came to court
He glimpsed among the crowd someone he thought

Was Azrael himself, now deathly grim
So from the crowd Suleiman summoned him

And asked Azrael why he had been cruel
And flashed extinction's gaze upon that fool.

Then Azrael said 'God instructed me
To take his life in the land of the three

Rivers known as Hind. That command was clear
So I was shocked to encounter him here.

Even if he turned into a swift bird
He'd not get there. I thought it was absurd

And the look on my face was of surprise.
Then there he was in Hind! We must surmise

That what God commands no one can gainsay
My job is not to question but obey!'

My friends, don't look to challenge destiny
What He tells angels (or us) has to be.

THE VALUE OF TEARS

By the side of a sandy desert road
A man, with his dog, had rested his load

Because the dog lay down, exhausted, dying
His master crouched over his dear pet, crying.

A beggar spotted them as he passed by
And asked the poor, wretched, weeping
man why

He was in this awful state of distress.
The man replied 'Here lies my happiness

My companion, he kept watch every night
And put thieves and bandits to abject flight

He would catch partridges and bring their meat
So I was never short of food to eat.'

The beggar then asked 'Now what's
wrong with him?'
'He's dying of hunger, a fate so grim!'

The beggar then asked 'So, what's in the sack?'
'Oh that's full of leftover food to pack

And carry for my next meal or next day
I have to save every bit on the way.'

'So why not give a little to your friend?
Assuage his hunger that'll put an end

To his plight and to your sorrow and your fears.'
'I can't,' the man said, 'I'm shedding these tears

Instead. You see these tears don't cost
And as I shed them I don't feel I've lost

Anything. Even scraps of food are worth
Something. Unlike tears that soak the earth.'

The beggar was disgusted and he cursed
The man. He felt this was by far the worst

Equation or comparison he'd heard
And went his way without a further word.

This beggar was right but disdained to teach
The fool the relative value of each.

These values caused his poor dog to be killed.
Tears are blood into water distilled.

Longing for change can fill one's eyes
with tears
They bring you Love and Freedom from
your fears.

ISSAH AND THE FOOL

Issah the Prophet was accompanied
By his apostles or someone in need

Of prophecies or comfort from His word.
On one journey a young man who had heard

Of Issah's powers joined his entourage
Because in truth he doubted, by and large

That Issah could do the things people said
They'd witnessed him do—like raising the dead.

As they journeyed, the young man thought he saw
Human bones in a ditch. Could he restore

Them back to life if Issah would impart
The resurrecting prayer? So this upstart

Accosted Issah saying 'Prophet, please
Teach me the secret prayer to restore these

Bones into a living being and prove
The Power that God gave you to remove

The pall of death from corpses and to heal
The wretched of the earth. Can you reveal

The secret words to me?' Issah ignored
This fool wanting the powers of the Lord.

This idiot repeated his bold request
Attempting to put Issah to the test.

Finally, Issah, in disgust replied:
'Foolish young man, only He can decide

To bestow such powers in the pure soul
Only the purest prophets can control

These miracles. The sinner who poses
With stone tablets doesn't become Moses!'

'Aha! So, that's the truth,' the upstart said,
'Even you can't restore this pile of dead

Bones to life.' Issah turned to God to ask
Had He sent this idiot to pose this task?

Then Issah was inspired with the Word
From God and in his head clearly heard

'These cynical idiots sow seeds of doubt
Their acts and thoughts will serve to find them out

The rose they thought their saviour turns to thorn
From their lover's bodies a snake is born

They have the gift of poison and instead
Of generating wealth turn gold to lead!'

Hearing this Issah thought 'I should fulfil
This idiot's demand, at the least that will

Prove the Word and Power of God survive
This cynic's test. The bones then came alive

When Issah whispered the prayer and then blew
The miraculous Power to renew

To life the bones. Bu Lo! The big surprise
Was that they rose, but not in human guise.

Confronting the young man was a big black
Lion who then proceeded to attack

The young cynic and tear him limb from limb
Was this God's punishment for doubting Him?

Then Issah asked this vengeful lion why
He'd killed this fool. 'After all I

Brought you back to life at his behest
Though that was a challenge, the doubter's test!'

'I killed him because he tried to defy
You, great Prophet Issah—and that is why

I won't treat him as my prey and devour
His flesh. Vultures and jackals will soon scour

This place for carrion—the price fools must pay.'
And so saying, the lion walked away.

IBRAHIM'S ENLIGHTENMENT

Ibrahim, King of Balkh was very rich
And had several indulgent habits which

Didn't detract from his reputation
As the fount of justice in the nation.

One night as Ibrahim slept in his bed
He woke to the sound of banging up ahead

It sounded as though it came from the roof
Persistent as though from a horse's hoof.

Had thieves climbed over the high palace wall?
So through the window he began to call

The palace guards. He shouted 'What the hell
Is going on?' The noise began to swell.

The banging became incredibly loud.
Lighting a lamp Ibrahim saw a crowd

He shouted out: 'In God's name, who are you?
The gates are guarded, how did you get through?'

'We're chasing camels, our entire herd!'
'What camels?' Asked Ibrahim, 'That's absurd!'

'The ones that have climbed on to your roof-top
Until they're down the pounding will not stop.'

'Don't be ridiculous,' Ibrahim said,
Thinking these foolish men have been misled.

'This is foolishness, please leave me alone.'
'As foolish as seeking God from a throne?'

Was the question they put to Ibrahim.
'All your wealth prevents you from
seeking Him!'

And hearing this Ibrahim gasped in awe
And quit his palace to return no more

He preached the word of God in Khorasan
The most respected Sufi in Iran

His story now is through the ages told
How absurdities can the Truth unfold.

MATERIAL IS IMMATERIAL

A woman who constantly sought to please
Her husband brought home a bag of chickpeas

To make his favourite dish of chickpea broth
A thick brown soup coated with bubbly froth

Or maybe a salad with olive oil
But first of all she knew she had to boil

The chickpeas in water and so prepare
Them for the family's evening fare.

The chickpeas were now bouncing up and down
Knowing that they would soften and
then drown

So from the pot they began to complain
'Why have you subjected us to such pain?

We were first harvested from where we grew
Dragged to the market and then bought by you

Torn from our roots we accepted it well
So why cast us into this fiery hell?'

The woman heard their pleading and she said
'Be calm, when you're thus transformed, you're not
dead

You were born to this universal plan
To nourish as food both woman and man.

Ultimately this universal whole
Decrees you nourish both body and soul

So chickpeas be content and realize
You live anew when your material dies.'

THE PEBBLE PARABLE

Arabian merchants from the distant past
Carried their goods to sell across the vast

Deserts of Arabia from east to west
And in desert oases took their rest

Their camels tied up in a caravan.
One of them came across a learned man

Who, approaching him in the oasis
And pointing to his camel, asked what this

Beast of burden carried on its back
The merchant said 'That's wheat in the left sack.'

'Then what's he carrying on the other side?'
'A sack of pebbles,' the merchant replied.

And with a grin he said 'You see the weight
Has to be balanced, my friend, that's no great

Feat of intellect, it's just what we do.'
The learned man said, 'My advice to you

Is empty out the pebble sack complete
And fill it with half the other sack's wheat.

That leaves the camel only half the weight
And you can travel at a faster rate.'

On hearing this the merchant was struck dumb
Why had he not worked out this simple sum?

'Who are you?' he asked, 'Are you a wise sage?
A king, a chieftain, master of our age?'

'No sir, I am nothing, look at my rags
My only clothes, no possessions, no bags.'

'You must have camels, cows or even sheep?'
'No sir, I have nothing, I even sleep

On the rough sand beneath the open sky
No home, no roof, I am a desert fly.'

'You must have hidden gold?' the merchant said.
'I have nothing, I even beg for bread!

My intelligence has brought me to this.
Wisdom is not the key to worldly bliss.'

'If that's true then please leave right away, go!
This "wisdom" may be infectious and so

Catching this disease will mean poverty.
Don't touch that sack of pebbles, let them be!'

The merchant then rode his camel away
Leaving Wisdom to starve another day.'

CONTROLLING ANGER

Issah the Prophet, to whom be all praise,
Was approached to illuminate God's ways

And constantly asked questions by disturbed
Individuals who'd value every word

Spoken by Issah. So one day a man
Approached him asking, 'Master, if you can

Set my heart at rest by telling me true
Human life is vain, what will ensue—

What is the worst that humans have to fear?'
So then in four words, all concise and clear

Issah replied '*The wrath of God*' that's all
That human's should fear after the fall

Of man's first disobedience and the fruit
Of that forbidden tree and the pursuit

Of sin. The man asked Issah 'how can we avoid
God's wrath? Tells us what grace can be employed

To assuage His wrath?' Issah replied
'Control your own wrath, let God be your guide!'

THE ONLY PLACE

Two lovers who were united at last
Met in a garden discussing their past

She asked him now he'd traversed many lands,
Seen monuments across the seas and sands

Which place or city would he say was best?
In every way—which one surpassed the rest?

Her lover had no need to hesitate
He gently grasped her and then he looked straight

Into her eyes. He answered with a smile
'There are beautiful places which beguile

The senses with their splendour and their scale
With avenues and buildings that prevail

Through ages and epochs, but still my choice
Is where in darkness I can hear your voice

If we were in the deepest darkest well
Or on the fiery road to gates of hell

If you were there that place would be my choice
Where love is—that's where two hearts can rejoice.'

SIZE MATTERS

A merchant who had travelled through the day
Found a caravanserai where he could lay

His tired limbs and rest his camel too
Which companion he left in haste undue.

The camel's bridle was left unsecured
Trailing the ground—a rope or unbound cord.

A mouse scuttling by thought she saw a snake
But getting close saw she'd made a mistake

Here was the rope that she could grasp to lead
A camel, like a desert lord indeed!

The mouse then got the bridle in her grip
The camel, quite amused, disdained to whip

The bridle rope from this small creature's paws
He welcomed this development because

Standing alone in the dark he was bored
And working for this merchant he endured

The relentless hard work and cruelty
If this mouse led him away he'd be free

The mouse now proudly thought she was in charge
Of a humble creature ever so large

And started leading him across the sand
Feeling puffed up with pride and very grand.

The camel thought it was best to ignore
This creature's conceit even though he saw

The mouse acting like she was in control—
While she scrambled he would leisurely stroll

Behind her. They soon came across a stream
A shallow creek but to her it would seem

A raging torrent, one she dare not cross
The camel asked her, 'What's the matter boss?

Why have we stopped, it's only just midday?'
'Look at this current, we'll be swept away.'

The poor mouse said. 'Humph', the camel sneered
'This little puddle? Don't be so weird!

Let's test it,' the camel said with a grin
And stepping to the bank he waded in.

He shouted 'Look it's just up to my knee
It's not so deep, come in and cross with me.'

The mouse then said, 'Oh camel, don't be daft
To get across I'd need a boat or raft

You stupid camel, consider my size
If we step in, then I'm the one who dies!'

The camel said, 'Why did you think it right
To lead a creature thousand times your height?

Why don't you keep the company of mice?
Does your ego tell you that won't suffice?'

The mouse said, 'You are right and I repent
I was led by conceit and I relent.'

The camel saw the mouse was at a loss
He said, 'Climb on my hump we'll get across.'

They crossed that stream and ever remained friends
And that is where this moral story ends.

You may not be a Prophet but you may
Arrive where they abide if you obey

The dictates of their prophecy and wait
In an attentive silence imitate

The questioning that makes you but an ear
The instrument that allows you to hear

The words which tell copper that it's not gold
Until it's transformed and the story's told.

REVELATION OF THE SCALES

A poor man married a greedy wife:
Food and wine were the focus of her life

She'd eat all he brought home and then she'd lie
About where the food went and she'd deny

Eating quantities she could not digest.
One day her husband invited a guest

And bought expensive lamb just for that meal
Trusting his greedy wife not to steal

This delicacy to buy which he'd slaved
For two hundred days during which he'd saved

What he earned so he could provide a feast
For his important guest, he thought at least

His greedy wife would hold off on this day.
He was, of course, wrong—while he was away

His wife cooked the lamb as kebabs and ate
The whole joint and then quickly washed the
plate

To wipe the evidence. The man came back
With his guest and spotted the empty rack

In the larder where the meat should have been.
'The cat's eaten the lamb, she's wiped it clean,'

She said. Her husband used to her tall tales
Sent his servant to fetch some weighing scales

And when they came he weighed the little cat
'Three pounds? The lamb was heavier
than that!

So was it really the cat who ate
The lamb? She would now be double her weight!

If this is the cat, then where's the meat?'
Like body and spirit they're not discrete

The spirit and the body both are one
Each is the other—no sums to be done!

Throw water at someone you make them wet
And dust hurled at them will not hurt—and yet

Combine the two to make a projectile
A lumpy brick, a hard, hurtful missile!

WHO EATS?

One year in a normally fertile land
The rains failed and so did crops. Nothing grew
Then famine raged, the population starved
A camel bull and ram, a motley crew

Decided they would scour the countryside
Looking for any greenery to eat.
They staggered about hungrily for days
Every green blade had withered in dry heat!

They searched by sniffing under every rock
Hoping some blades of grass would be alive
In their shadow protected from the sun
But soon realized that nothing could survive

The arid heat. But just as they despaired
Their luck changed and they found a fresh green
weed
On the wall of a damp and sheltered cave
But it was scraggy, not enough to feed

The three of them, so they had to decide
Which one would eat and leave the two without.
At least the one who ate would stay alive
Leaving the two to starve, they had no doubt.

So how was this decision to be made?
The ram then said 'The eldest is most frail
Respecting elders is what we should do
So, compare ages and let age prevail.

The ram then volunteered that he would start
By telling them his age he said 'I am
The twin brother of the biblical ram
Sacrificed by the Prophet Abraham

Instead of his son Ishmael.' The bull
Then interjected saying that he was
The husband of the cow that Adam used
To plough his fields. 'And so I've won because

Adam being the first person on earth
His cow and I are much older than all
The animals born later.' The camel
Knew that these were blatant lies and being tall

He reached the weed growing out of the side
Of the rocky cave. He said, 'I've no need
To be ancient like you and question luck.'
And so saying, he plucked and ate the weed

Leaving the other two to realize
That desperation shouldn't foster lies.

Aphorisms

I shall wait patiently from hour to hour
To hear the word from you which will empower
My humble self to be worthy of you
And for our love to blossom into a flower

When your thoughts turn to worry and you're
fraught
Think of the One who created all thought.

O give up all distraction, do not stray
It's only when your feet are on the way
That destinations become all too clear
The Path of Righteousness will self-display.

When you pray to the Sun and its bright light
You praise your own eyes and the gift of sight.

What hurts the heart can also make you whole
Darkness can be the candle of your soul.

By being still you'll know the dancer's worth
To know stillness, dance till you leave the earth.

Don't crawl through life like some low worm who clings
To mud and clay—you were gifted with wings!

Light your lantern, you are not just one
You are a thousand lights, bright as the Sun.

Why remain imprisoned in dark, why hide?
Step into the light, the door's open wide!

We have thought of it as rain through the years
Does heaven's veil conceal these angels' tears?

The wisdom of your books is as nothing
The answer lies within the questioning.

Anxiety for peace will bring you none
Disharmony will set that fretting sun.

O builder let eternal truth be told
The new is built on ruins of the old.

Don't knock on all these variegated doors
Knock on your heart's and that will open yours.

Demolish with your axe the prison wall
Become all space and sky—infinite all!

I dropped my hat while gazing at the moon
The gazing that induced my mind to swoon.

Sorrow is the broom that sweeps in joy
As autumn does the summer's leaves destroy
Making way for the rebirth of new springs
And to the bough of your heart greenness brings.

The meeting of friends is the sunny hour
Friendship is as spring rain to the flower.

I only want the presence of my friends
Only in friendship time dissolves and ends.

The world, my friends, is no more than a dream
However real to sleepers it may seem
Then death awakes the sleeper like the dawn
And all the grief from life's sad vale is gone.

The diamond of expressions is a smile
Especially from features infantile.

Ask the hand of sorrow to unfurl
God has placed in that palm a precious pearl.

Your insolence and refusal to praise
Him will keep you depressed for all your days.

Where am I and who was I meant to be?
A single wave located in the sea?

A marvel is the sight of souls we see
Behind the bars within their grasp the key!

Don't shun the ruin, you'll find that is where
Many a treasure entrusted to its care

Love is the sustenance of earthly things
If you live in the sky don't fold your wings

A sincere prayer clears the thickest mist
Restores the peace by which a soul is kissed.

O seeker, the emptiness of the void
Will leave this accidental world destroyed
Emptiness in your loves can bring you peace
And from the sickened heart provide release
The trickery of the word is life's stress
O seeker save your soul through emptiness!

Dance till your frenzied feet tread the soft air
Surrender heart and soul while you're up there

If words offend stay silent and content
As silence is a form of fulfilment.

You look upon the world and see it whole
It actually resides within your soul!

Let not your thoughts cast shadows on your heart
Expel your thoughts—at least keep them apart

You are the sun expelling darkness now
What need to wear that tiara on your brow?

Show me thy face, I crave the orchard's fruit;
Open thy lips mine own shall remain mute;
O lift the veil your radiance needs no shroud;
I crave the light, so Heavens, shift the cloud.

I am not flesh or blood, I am not skin
I'm the eternal soul that lives within.

O seek and find the barriers within
You erected against the love you crave
Demolish those if you intend to win
The battle to be The Beloved's slave.

When someone beats a rug using a broom
They've nothing against the rug—we presume
The blows are aimed at expelling the dust
And lay the revived rug back in their room.

Wisdom tells us that we are not worthy
Only Love can assure us that we are
The one leaves you feeling you are earthy
The other elevates you to a star.

Our yesterdays have melted with the springs
Today is new so say, please say, new things!

When you're thirsty you know water calls
Is the voice of water in waterfalls?

No need to travel, journey within and wait
In yourself, which mines of rubies illuminate.

Song and dance, laughter and sweet wine
Are paths I have chosen to the Divine.

When I first heard a love story I knew
My life had to be spent looking for you.

I give myself to you and become yours
Don't give me back myself, my heart implores.

TRANSLATOR'S NOTE

My maternal uncle and my father both studied Persian in school. My father let his knowledge lapse and picked it up again when he went to work in Isfahan to set up a steel plant for the Shah's government. Older members up the family tree also studied Persian.

My great-grandfather, my paternal grandmother's father, Jamshed Saklatwala devoted his time to Persian scholarship. He translated Omar Khayyam's *Rubaiyat*, a copy of which is still in the family. He is also supposed to have translated a selection of Rumi's verses. His published translation of Rumi is lost to posterity. Perhaps no great loss, I can't say.

He translated Omar Khayyam into English and claims in the Foreword to his translation that he has read Fitzgerald's effort but deems it not to be accurate or true in detail to the verses. I have, of course, compared my ancestor's version with that of Edward Fitzgerald's and have to admit that the latter wins by a long chalk. Jamshedji's translation, though faithful to the rhyme-scheme of the rubaii and to its metre, doesn't compare. Its literality interferes with the imagery and there is no music to the verse as there is in the enchanting compulsion in Fitzgerald's. If something is lost in translation, the loss is balanced by an enhanced beauty and an overall faithfulness to the Sufi scepticism which Khayyam may have propounded.

Growing up in India, in a Parsi Zoroastrian family, I had heard constantly of Rumi the poet without having heard any of his work. No circumstance or reference bred any sort of curiosity in me about it. He remained as closed a book as one of those from the Old Testament whose names I knew but whose content I had never bothered to access. It was on a trip from Mumbai to Australia that I was first introduced to modern translations of Rumi in English. My friend Sorab Irani, who gave me a lift to the airport for my trip, presented me with an anthology of Rumi's verse in translation. It was a translation by an American called Coleman Barks. I hadn't carried any reading material with me in my hand luggage so was grateful for the gift.

As I settled into the flight, I opened the book and began to read the verses. The first few, without metre or rhyme and certainly without the music that haunts the free verse of Walt Whitman or T.S. Eliot, struck me as prosaic nonsense. I read on. It was a long flight from Mumbai to Brisbane and stopped for a while in Singapore.

Some of the verse struck me as obscure and even in its obscurity as chopped-up prose rather than poetry. I told myself that this must be the prevalent form of contemporary verse and was probably acknowledged in some circles as extremely proficient poetry. It was my biased limitation, demanding from 'poetry' the satisfactions I was used to from Shakespeare through Keats to Yeats and even to the Indian poets such as, Adil Jussawala, Dom Moraes, Jeet Thayil and twenty others to whose work I regularly turn.

I reproduce the sort of verse from Mr Barks's translations that had me bewildered:

Go to your pillow and sleep, my son
Leave me alone in the passion
Of this death-night

Fair enough—I suppose death-night means it's very dark.

But then the poem goes on to say:

Let the mill turn with your grieving,
But stay clear. Don't fall

Into the river with me.
There's no way out
No cure but death …

The translation ends mysteriously with:

Bahauddin my son,
If you want to be impressively learned
Memorize a famous historian
And quote him as someone else.

Obviously, millions of readers in the USA bought this stuff. On the plane to Brisbane, I was disappointed and frustrated that I didn't know why or how one could 'memorize a historian and quote him as someone else'.

The story goes that Coleman Barks, a disciple of someone called Robert Bly, was handed a copy of Rumi translations by the great Cambridge orientalist, scholar of Persian, A.J. Arberry, and told to 'liberate' the verse from Arberry's diligent scholarly work.

Bly, whoever he is or was, probably meant that Barks should turn Arberry's masterful Victorian or Georgian style translations into 1970's American argot. The conceit is astounding. Arberry, following his mentor and Cambridge orientalist R. Nicholson, pioneered the accurate Sufi translations of Rumi's verse. They may not have been the poets that Fitzgerald was, but they embraced the accuracy of the religious meanings of Rumi's masterful output and respected its poetic forms.

This Robert Bly's injunction to Mr Barks to Americanize Rumi's verse, has indeed projected the thirteenth century's poet to be the most read in the USA. There is nothing sacred or even legally copyrighted about Rumi's volumes of verse. 'Translators' may, with impunity, trade on the needs and supply the 'spiritual' solace that contemporary readers may want to gain from Rumi's monumental and strictly Sufi-Islamic verse.

On that flight I put the book aside and, apart from drinking a Bloody Mary that the air hostess offered me, slept till we landed at the Brisbane airport.

On my return to Mumbai after a few weeks in Australia, I was living in the flat of my maternal uncle. He saw the Rumi translations and asked me if I'd been reading it. I said words to the effect that I found Rumi's verse not to my taste. In fact, I might have said it is a load of mixed metaphors and chopped-up nonsensical prose. My mamaji, my mother's brother, was absolutely appalled. His reaction was: 'How dare you!'

And he immediately went into a recitation in Persian of what must have been one of his favourite verses. I listened.

'Mamaji, please say that again,' I requested.

He repeated the verses at greater length as I listened.

'Iambic pentameter,' I said.

'What's that?' Mamu asked.

'It's the pattern of the verse—a dum, a dum, a dum, a dum, a dum. Shakespeare used it, but that was three hundred years after Rumi. And the verse rhymes.'

'Of course, it rhymes. It's poetry!' Mamu said.

I asked him to translate. We sat into the night as he did. I took notes. When he went to bed, I sat up attempting to turn the translations into rhyming and iambic pentametric verse.

I implored Mamaji to recite or read more of Rumi's poetry to me the next day and for the weeks following. It was my first attempt at Rumi and the verses readily found a publisher in India and the USA.

As I worked on the 'translations', I accessed and read books on Rumi's life, on the Cambridge translators R. Nicholson and Arberry. Through a trick of fate, the name A.J. Arberry was immediately evocative. When I went up in the mid nineteen-sixties to study Natural Sciences at Pembroke College, Cambridge, his name graced a staircase leading to his rooms in the first of the three courts of the college. I remembered the frail, short figure of the professor walking in a long coat with a walking stick through the courts of the college. I didn't realize then who he was, apart from having gathered that he was the senior-most fellow in residence and a distinguished Orientalist scholar.

'Translation' is normally understood as the conveyance of thought from one language to another. It is, of course, much more complex when the language from which one renders a contemporary 'translation' exists in another epoch and another culture with its assumptions that may have been unique to itself. Rumi's verse is in Persian with Arabic and Turkish insertions at times. His thirteenth-century Persian doesn't differ all that much from contemporary Persian and anyone who speaks the language, especially those who are not Persian but have acquired the language through literary studies, can easily discern the meanings of its sentences. The interpretation of its metaphors, of its imagery and other constructs which are dependent on a cultural understanding may indeed get lost in translation.

Deepak Chopra, Director of the Chopra Centre for Well-being in California has published his translation of Rumi's love poems. They are by all accounts popular and the singer Madonna has used them as lyrics for her songs.

Franklin D. Lewis, in his comprehensive, scholarly *Rumi: Past and Present, East and West* writes:

> *Chopra evidently did not spend much time learning about Rumi's life; not only does the book* (Love Poems of Rumi) *fail to introduce the reader to the name of Shams, it reflects confusion about the century in which Rumi lived. At the end of the introduction we read that Rumi's teachings 'live on one thousand years after he walked on this earth', though poor Rumi has only been in the ground for 725 years.*

Lewis expresses his criticism of the 'translations': 'As such, they have far more to do with Chopra's New Age garrulity (or guru-ality) than with Rumi's Shams-fired Muslim mysticism.'

He also notes that apart from attracting Madonna to sing the lyrics, Chopra's 'translations' have 'moved Rumi into the glamorous world of high fashion. Designer Donna Karan, describing herself as enamoured of light, introduced her new fall fashions, inspired by none other than the love poems of Rumi. Her models sauntered down the runway (sic) accompanied by a soundtrack with readings from Deepak's versions of Rumi by such discerning mystics and literary connoisseurs as Madonna and Demi Moore.'

Chopra's book includes the text of four translations by Coleman Barks, who, Lewis writes, 'in a gesture of mutual admiration, has contributed a testimonial blurb for the dust jacket.'

Professor Lewis is not enamoured or amused.

This is my third collection of translations. I've said that the first was occasioned by my maternal uncle's indignation at my negative response to Rumi's work after reading translations which, whatever else they were, didn't fit the definition of poetry as I knew it.

Subsequently, I relied on the literal translations from the Persian of my friend Firdaus Ali, who was familiar with classical and contemporary Persian.

Using his word-for-word English and occasionally Urdu renditions (he wrote them all up in his very decorative calligraphic hand in cheap, lined notebooks) and referring to the work of Arberry and Nicholson on the same poems, I arrived at the verses in this selection.

Unable to recreate, even in sympathetic conscience, the cultural impact of Rumi's words, which belong in his time, I have no pretence of being totally faithful to his meanings but have attempted to retain the metre and convey in English the rhyme of his strictly formal constructions. The contemporary reader will, of course, know that his references to 'wine' are metaphors for the spirit that transforms, that love and union are not expressions of sexual desire, but rather metaphors for the union of spirits that are dedicated to the quest for the Infinite.

ABOUT THE TRANSLATOR

Farrukh Dhondy is a British-Indian writer born in Pune in 1944. He went to school and college in India and then on a scholarship to Cambridge University. He is a writer of fiction, non-fiction, stage and TV plays, films, biographies, translations and journalism. His recent autobiography is called *Fragments Against My Ruin.*

HarperCollins *Publishers* India

At HarperCollins India, we believe in telling the best stories and finding the widest readership for our books in every format possible. We started publishing in 1992; a great deal has changed since then, but what has remained constant is the passion with which our authors write their books, the love with which readers receive them, and the sheer joy and excitement that we as publishers feel in being a part of the publishing process.

Over the years, we've had the pleasure of publishing some of the finest writing from the subcontinent and around the world, including several award-winning titles and some of the biggest bestsellers in India's publishing history. But nothing has meant more to us than the fact that millions of people have read the books we published, and that somewhere, a book of ours might have made a difference.

As we look to the future, we go back to that one word—a word which has been a driving force for us all these years.

Read.

Harper Collins · 4th · HARPER FICTION · HARPER NON-FICTION · HARPER BUSINESS · HCCB HARPERCOLLINS CHILDREN'S BOOKS

HARPER DESIGN · Harper Sport · HARPER PERENNIAL · HARPER VANTAGE · हार्पर हिन्दी